Henry Lucas

Songs of Zion by Hebrew Singers of Mediaeval Times

Henry Lucas

Songs of Zion by Hebrew Singers of Mediaeval Times

ISBN/EAN: 9783744775915

Printed in Europe, USA, Canada, Australia, Japan

Cover: Foto ©Lupo / pixelio.de

More available books at **www.hansebooks.com**

Songs of Zion by Hebrew Singers of Mediæval Times

Translated into English Verse by Mrs. Henry Lucas

London : Published by J. M. DENT and Co. at Aldine House in Great Eastern Street 1894

CONTENTS

		PAGE
I. ODE TO ZION, . . . *Jehuda Halevi,*		1
II. 'GOD! WHOM SHALL I COMPARE TO THEE?' *Jehuda Halevi,*		6
III. SERVANT OF GOD (Hymn for the Day of Atonement), ... *Jehuda Halevi,*		9
IV. MY KING (Hymn for New Year), *Moses b. Nachman,*		13
V. TO THE SOUL, . . *Jehuda Halevi,*		16
VI. SABBATH HYMN, . *Shelomo Halevi,*		18
VII. O SLEEPER! WAKE, ARISE! . *Jehuda Halevi,*		20
VIII. THE LAND OF PEACE, . *Solomon ibn Gebirol,*		24
IX. THE HEART'S DESIRE (Hymn for the Day of Atonement), . . . *Jehuda Halevi,*		26
X. O SOUL, WITH STORMS BESET! *Solomon ibn Gebirol,*		29
XI. SANCTIFICATION, *Joseph ibn Abitur,*		33

CONTENTS

			PAGE
XII.	HYMN OF PRAISE, . . *Abraham ibn Ezra*,		39
XIII.	PASSOVER HYMN, . . *Jehuda Halevi*,		41
XIV.	MORNING PRAYER, . . *Jehuda Halevi*,		44
XV.	JUDGMENT AND MERCY (Hymn for New Year),		45
XVI.	GRACE AFTER MEALS, ...		48
XVII.	'LORD OF THE UNIVERSE,'		51
XVIII.	HYMN FOR THE CONCLUSION OF THE SABBATH,		53
XIX.	GOD AND MAN, . . . *Jehuda Halevi*,		56
XX.	HYMN FOR TABERNACLES, *Eleazar b. Jacob Kalir*,		60
XXI.	HYMN FOR PENTECOST, . . *Jehuda Halevi*,		62
XXII.	HYMN OF GLORY, ...		63
XXIII.	HYMN OF UNITY FOR THE SEVEN DAYS OF THE WEEK, ...		66
XXIV.	PENITENTIAL PRAYER, . *Moses ibn Ezra*,		71
XXV.	THE LIVING GOD WE PRAISE, . . .		75

INTRODUCTION

THE originals of the following poems are, with one or two exceptions, to be found in the Sabbath and festival prayer-books in use in the synagogues of English and foreign Jewish communities. By far the larger number come to us from mediæval Spain, where Hebrew poetry reached the highest point of devotional and poetical excellence. There the Jewish hymnologists were alike poets and philosophers, and the stream of learning and cultivation, mingling with that of poetry, flowed through the plains of religious life and enriched them in a thousand ways, while the fruit of the tree of knowledge was used both to enlighten and strengthen religious faith, and to adorn and beautify divine service.

INTRODUCTION

For some centuries after Judea ceased to be a separate state, Hebrew poetry remained as it had been in Bible times, *i.e.* unrhymed and undivided into lines and stanzas.

But little by little the Spanish Jews became acquainted with the poetry of the Arabs, and the natural result was the adoption of rhyme, and later still of stanzas, often elaborately arranged. The originals of all the following translations are rhymed —some in couplets, some in stanzas; but it has seldom been found possible to reproduce with absolute exactness the verse-arrangement of the Hebrew, as to the number of lines and rhymes in each stanza. It is impossible to say with certainty when rhyme first appeared in Hebrew poetry, still less can it be ascertained when the stanza became part of it; but both are to be found in the writings of Eleazar b. Jacob Kalir, who lived about the middle of the tenth century, probably in the south of Italy. His style is terse, and often obscure, crowded with images, complicated by new forms of words and phrases, and frequently rendered artificial by involved versification, rhymes, and

INTRODUCTION

acrostics, but full of poetic fervour and enthusiasm. He composed upwards of two hundred poems for divine service, many of which are still retained in the liturgies of French, German, and Italian Jews.

Kalir's compositions became the general type and model of Jewish hymnology, until towards the middle of the following century, when Hebrew poetry, in Spain at least, took a higher and more unfettered flight.

Among a number of more or less well-known poets four shine out with especial lustre: these four are Solomon Ibn Gebirol, Moses Ibn Ezra, Abraham Ibn Ezra, and, greatest of all, Jehuda Halevi. All four were philosophers as well as poets, but their poetical works are all that need be mentioned here.

Solomon Ibn Gebirol (b. 1021) was a native of Malaga. His parents died early, and appear to have left him without means. It is uncertain when he left Malaga for Saragossa, but we hear of him in the latter place as enjoying the protection of Jekutiel Ibn Hassan, who held a high position in that town under King Jachya Ibn Moudair. But a rebellion, which cast the king from the throne, cost Jekutiel his life, and Gebirol his patron, a loss which he lamented in a touching elegy of more than two hundred verses. This elegy was far from being Gebirol's first poetic flight: his earliest known poem was composed in his nineteenth year, and consisted of a Hebrew grammar in verse, in which his extraordinary fluency and ease of diction triumphs even over the dry difficulties of his subject. All his poems, both secular and religious, are distinguished by their flowing and harmonious verse. Those that treat of his personal fortune and feelings are of a melancholy and somewhat egotistic tone, but his liturgic poems are full of the purest and loftiest religious thought. Among them are to be found every variety of religious poetry, hymns of praise and penitence, thanksgivings, lamentations and prayers for fasts and feasts. But his best known and most important composition is the series of half religious, half philosophical poems, called 'Keter Malchut' (Crown of Sovereignty) in which he pours forth all his thoughts on religion, all his speculations, all his ardent love of and gratitude to God, besides all that he has learned

INTRODUCTION

from the theology of his own nation, and the science and wisdom of the age in which he lived. Few further details are known of Ibn Gebirol's life. It is said that the first persecution of the Jews in Spain since its conquest by Islam (the attack on Joseph Ibn Nagrela and his Jewish fellow-citizens in Granada, 1066) embittered the last years of the poet, and he died after many wanderings, in the year 1070, in Valencia.

Moses Ibn Ezra was the second and most distinguished of four brothers Ibn Ezra of Granada, who were all learned and wealthy. The dates both of his birth and death are uncertain, but the former is supposed to be about 1070, the latter 1139. An unfortunate attachment appears to have first aroused his muse, and like Ibn Gebirol his secular poems are chiefly occupied with describing his own feelings and bewailing his own fate. As a religious poet he was extraordinarily prolific, and his penitential poems ('Selichot') are especially numerous. He had a wonderful command of language, and enriched Hebrew poetry with a variety of metres, but the very interest he took in the form of his verse has sometimes an unfavourable effect on its contents, and his poems have neither the spontaneity of Gebirol nor the majesty of Halevi. His penitential hymns, however, show much earnestness of feeling and poetic enthusiasm. He was held in high honour by his contemporaries, and Jehuda Halevi, with whom he had been on friendly terms, and with whom he corresponded for years, wrote a touching tribute to his memory.[1]

Abraham Ibn Ezra (born about 1088, died 1167) was at once theologian, philosopher, commentator, grammarian, mathematician, traveller, and poet. It must, however, be confessed that he was too much of a critical philosopher[2] to be a true poet. His religious poems are not so much hymns as a series of reflections on the high destiny of man, whom God has endowed with thought and intellect, and who ought therefore to use these gifts in His service. But the elevated tone and strong religious feeling of Ibn Ezra's poems give him an honourable place among the poets of his nation, while his extra-

[1] See Graetz, *History of the Jews.*
[2] Sach, *History of the Religious Poetry of the Jews in Spain.*

INTRODUCTION

ordinarily varied talents, and the adventures of his wandering life, make him too interesting a figure to be passed over in silence. His early life was spent in Toledo, but want of means compelled him to seek a livelihood elsewhere. He was, however, not destined to be wealthy, and he declared quaintly, that if he 'took to candle-making as a trade, the sun would never set again until the hour of his death.' His wanderings led him by turns to Italy, France, Egypt, Palestine, and England. During his sojourn in London in the course of 1158, he wrote a treatise called 'Yesod Moreh' (Foundation of Religion), which he dedicated to Jacob Ben Joseph of London, and also his 'Sabbath Epistle,' which he says he wrote 'in one of the cities of the island called the "corner of the earth" (Angleterre), for it is in the last of the seven divisions of the inhabited earth.'[1] He continued his wandering life for many years, and died at Calahorra on the borders of Navarre and Aragon.

Jehuda Halevi, the greatest Hebrew poet of Spain, or indeed of any other country since the Psalmists,

[1] See *The Jews of Angevin England*, J. Jacobs.

was born in Old Castile in 1086. His life presents no very striking incidents. After studying at the college of Lucena, he decided on adopting the medical profession, and became a physician on returning to Toledo, his native place. Here he practised many years, and appears to have been highly esteemed as a doctor, for he writes to a friend that 'the city is large, and that he is busily engaged curing the illness of the inhabitants.' But he longed, he says in the same letter, for the time when he may depart and 'seek some place of living knowledge, the fountain of wisdom.'[1] All his life he had been filled with a passionate desire to visit the Holy Land, and at last (about 1140) he bade farewell to his only daughter, his grandson, and a large circle of friends and pupils, and started on his pilgrimage. His poems, describing the perils of the journey, and especially of the sea voyage, are overflowing with the finest poetic imagery, but most beautiful of all is his 'Ode to Zion,' which, according to tradition, he composed at the very gates of Jerusalem. The legend tells how, while he was

[1] See Graetz, *History of the Jews.*

INTRODUCTION

reciting it, an Arab soldier rode over him and killed him, just as he was about to set foot in the holy city. It is, however, more than probable that he never came even thus near the goal of his desires, but that he died on the journey from Egypt to Palestine.

Jehuda Halevi has enriched the Jewish liturgy with at least three hundred poems, for the celebration of the various fasts and feasts of the Jewish calendar. Their flowing and harmonious verse, and the mastery displayed in them over the pure Hebrew of the Bible is only a small part of their attractions; the wonderful mingling of religious fervour with the true spirit of poetry is what constitutes their inner charm, of which, it is to be hoped, traces may still be found even in a translation. A strong national spirit pervades his poetry, and when, in his 'Songs of Zion,' he sings of the past and future glories of Jerusalem, and mourns over her present sorrows, his muse rises to a height which may not unfitly be compared even to the Psalms. Heine, in his delightful, but utterly untranslatable, fragment 'Jehuda Ben Halevy,' dwells especially on this tendency, and tells how the poet, like all other minstrels of his time, loved a fair lady, whom he celebrated in his verse.

> ' But a wan and woeful maiden
> Was his love: a mournful image
> Of despair and desolation,
> Who was named Jerusalem.
>
> Even in his early boyhood
> Did he love her, deeply, truly,
> And a thrill of passion shook him
> At the word Jerusalem.'

And the 'Ode to Zion' is thus described :—

> 'Tears of pearl, that on the golden
> Thread of rhyme are strung together,
> From the shining forge of poetry
> Have come forth in song celestial.
>
> And this is the song of Zion,
> That Jehuda ben Halevy
> Sang when dying on the holy
> Ruins of Jerusalem.'

No star of similar magnitude has risen on the Jewish horizon since Jehuda Halevi's 'pillar of fire' vanished from the scene, but many lesser lights pierced the darkness of the Middle Ages, and brightened the pages of the old Machsors (prayer-books) in times of anxiety and persecution, when the synagogue service gave the only touch of light and colour, of peace and gladness. But with the end of the twelfth century the golden age of Hebrew poetry ended likewise. Moses ben Nachman (born about 1195, died about 1270) may be cited as the author of a truly magnificent poem for the New Year festival, and here and there in the course of the three following centuries, an otherwise unknown name appears as the writer of some well-known hymn, as for instance the familiar 'Sabbath Hymn' by R. Shelomo Halevi, who is said to have lived at Safet in the sixteenth century. But the days of Solomon Gebirol and Jehuda Halevi were past and gone, and Hebrew poetry, after three centuries of song, has again sunk to silence, from which it seems little likely to be aroused.

I

Ode to Zion

Art thou not, Zion, fain
To send forth greetings from thy sacred rock
Unto thy captive train,
Who greet thee as the remnants of thy flock?
Take thou on every side—
East, west, and south, and north—their greetings
    multiplied.
Sadly he greets thee still,
The prisoner of hope, who, day and night,
Sheds ceaseless tears, like dew on Hermon's hill—
Would that they fell upon thy mountain's height!

Harsh is my voice when I bewail thy woes,
But when in fancy's dream
I see thy freedom, forth its cadence flows
Sweet as the harps that hung by Babel's stream.
My heart is sore distressed
For Bethel ever blessed,

For Peniel, and each ancient, sacred place.
The holy presence there
To thee is present where
Thy Maker opes thy gates, the gates of heaven to face.

The glory of the Lord will ever be
Thy sole and perfect light;
No need hast thou, then, to illumine thee,
Of sun by day, or moon and stars by night.
I would that, where God's Spirit was of yore
Poured out unto thy holy ones, I might
There too my soul outpour!
The house of kings and throne of God wert thou,
How comes it then that now
Slaves fill the throne where sat thy kings before?

O! who will lead me on
To seek the spots where, in far-distant years,
The angels in their glory dawned upon
Thy messengers and seers?
O! who will give me wings
That I may fly away,
And there, at rest from all my wanderings,

ODE TO ZION

The ruins of my heart among thy ruins lay?
I'll bend my face unto thy soil, and hold
Thy stones as precious gold.
And when in Hebron I have stood beside
My fathers' tombs, then will I pass in turn
Thy plains and forest wide,
Until I stand on Gilead and discern
Mount Hor and Mount Abarim, 'neath whose crest
Thy luminaries twain, thy guides and beacons rest.

Thy air is life unto my soul, thy grains
Of dust are myrrh, thy streams with honey flow;
Naked and barefoot, to thy ruined fanes
How gladly would I go;
To where the ark was treasured, and in dim
Recesses dwelt the holy cherubim.

I rend the beauty of my locks, and cry
In bitter wrath against the cruel fate
That bids thy holy Nazarites to lie
In earth contaminate.

How can I make or meat or drink my care,
How can mine eyes enjoy
The light of day, when I see ravens tear
Thy eagles' flesh, and dogs thy lions' whelps destroy?
Away! thou cup of sorrow's poisoned gall!
Scarce can my soul thy bitterness sustain.
When I Ahola unto mind recall,
I taste thy venom; and when once again
Upon Aholiba I muse, thy dregs I drain.

Perfect in beauty, Zion! how in thee
Do love and grace unite!
The souls of thy companions tenderly
Turn unto thee; thy joy was their delight,
And, weeping, they lament thy ruin now.
In distant exile, for thy sacred height
They long, and towards thy gates in prayer they bow.
Thy flocks are scattered o'er the barren waste,
Yet do they not forget thy sheltering fold,
Unto thy garments' fringe they cling, and haste
The branches of thy palms to seize and hold.

ODE TO ZION

Shinar and Pathros! come they near to thee?
Nought are they by thy Light and Right divine.
To what can be compared the majesty
Of thy anointed line?
To what the singers, seers, and Levites thine?
The rule of idols fails and is cast down,
Thy power eternal is, from age to age thy crown.

The Lord desires thee for his dwelling-place
Eternally; and blest
Is he whom God has chosen for the grace
Within thy courts to rest.
Happy is he that watches, drawing near,
Until he sees thy glorious lights arise,
And over whom thy dawn breaks full and clear
Set in the orient skies.
But happiest he, who, with exultant eyes,
The bliss of thy redeemed ones shall behold,
And see thy youth renewed as in the days of old.

JEHUDA HALEVI.

II

'God! Whom shall I compare to Thee?'

God! whom shall I compare to Thee,
When Thou to none canst likened be?
Under what image shall I dare
To picture Thee, when ev'rywhere
All Nature's forms Thine impress bear?

Greater, O Lord! Thy glories are
Than all the heavenly chariot far.
Whose mind can grasp Thy world's design?
Whose word can fitly Thee define?
Whose tongue set forth Thy powers divine?

Can heart approach, can eye behold
Thee in Thy righteousness untold?
Whom didst Thou to Thy counsel call,
When there was none to speak withal
Since Thou wast first and Lord of all?

GOD! WHOM SHALL I COMPARE TO THEE?

Thy world eternal witness bears
That none its Maker's glory shares.
Thy wisdom is made manifest
In all things formed by Thy behest,
All with Thy seal's clear mark imprest.

Before the pillars of the sky
Were raised, before the mountains high
Were wrought, ere hills and dales were known,
Thou in Thy majesty alone
Didst sit, O God! upon Thy throne!

Hearts, seeking Thee, from search refrain,
And weary tongues their praise restrain.
Thyself unbound by time and place,
Thou dost pervade, support, embrace
The world and all created space.

The sages' minds bewildered grow,
The lightning speed of thought is slow.
'Awful in praises' art Thou named;
Thou fillest, strong in strength proclaimed,
This universe Thy hand has framed.

8 GOD! WHOM SHALL I COMPARE TO THEE?

Deep, deep beyond all fathoming,
Far, far beyond all measuring,
We can but seek Thy deeds alone;
When bow Thy saints before Thy throne
Then is Thy faithfulness made known.

Thy righteousness we can discern,
Thy holy law proclaim and learn.
Is not Thy presence near alway
To them who penitently pray,
But far from those who sinning stray?

Pure souls behold Thee, and no need
Have they of light: they hear and heed
Thee with the mind's keen ear, although
The ear of flesh be dull and slow.
Their voices answer to and fro.

Thy holiness for ever they proclaim:
The Lord of Hosts! thrice holy is His name!

JEHUDA HALEVI.

III

SERVANT OF GOD

O! would that I might be
A servant unto Thee,
Thou God by all adored:
Then, though by friends out-cast,
Thy hand would hold me fast,
And draw me near to Thee, my King and Lord.

Spirit and flesh are Thine,
O Heavenly Shepherd mine!
My hopes, my thoughts, my fears, Thou seest all,
Thou measurest my path, my steps dost know.
When Thou upholdest, who can make me fall?
When Thou restrainest, who can bid me go?
O! would that I might be
A servant unto Thee,

Thou God, by all adored.
Then, though by friends out-cast,
Thy hand would hold me fast,
And draw me near to Thee, my King and Lord!

Fain would my heart come nigh
To Thee, O God! on high,
But evil thoughts have led me far astray
From the pure path of righteous government.
Guide Thou me back into Thy holy way,
And count me not as one impenitent.
O! would that I might be
A servant unto Thee,
Thou God, by all adored.
Then, though by friends out-cast,
Thy hand would hold me fast,
And draw me near to Thee, my King and Lord!

If in my youth I still
Fail to perform Thy will,
What can I hope when age shall chill my breast?
Heal me, O Lord! with Thee is healing found—

Cast me not off, by weight of years opprest,
Forsake me not when age my strength has bound.
O! would that I might be
A servant unto Thee,
Thou God, by all adored.
Then, though by friends out-cast,
Thy hand would hold me fast,
And draw me near to Thee, my King and Lord!

Contrite and full of dread,
I mourn each moment fled
Midst idle follies roaming desolate;
I sink beneath transgressions manifold,
That from Thy presence keep me separate;
Nor can sin-darkened eyes Thy light behold.
O! would that I might be
A servant unto Thee,
Thou God, by all adored.
Then, though by friends out-cast,
Thy hand would hold me fast,
And draw me near to Thee, my King and Lord!

SERVANT OF GOD

So lead me that I may
Thy sovereign will obey.
Make pure my heart to seek Thy truth divine;
When burns my wound, be Thou with healing near!
Answer me, Lord! for sore distress is mine,
And say unto Thy servant, I am here!
O! would that I might be
A servant unto Thee,
Thou God, by all adored!
Then, though by friends out-cast,
Thy hand would hold me fast,
And draw me near to Thee, my King and Lord!

JEHUDA HALEVI.

IV

MY KING

Ere time began, ere age to age had thrilled,
I waited in His storehouse, as He willed;
He gave me being, but, my years fulfilled,
   I shall be summoned back before the King.

He called the hidden to the light of day,
To right and left, each side the fountain lay,
From out the stream and down the steps, the way
   That led me to the garden of the King.

Thou gavest me a light my path to guide,
To prove my heart's recesses still untried;
And as I went, Thy voice in warning cried:
   'Child! fear thou Him Who is thy God and King!'

True weight and measure learned my heart from Thee;
If blessings follow, then what joy for me!
If nought but sin, all mine the shame must be,
    For that was not determined by the King.

I hasten, trembling, to confess the whole
Of my transgressions, ere I reach the goal
Where mine own words must witness 'gainst my soul,
    And who dares doubt the writing of the King?

Erring, I wandered in the wilderness,
In passion's grave nigh sinking powerless:
Now deeply I repent, in sore distress,
    That I kept not the statutes of the King!

With worldly longings was my bosom fraught,
Earth's idle toys and follies all I sought;
Ah! when He judges joys so dearly bought,
    How greatly shall I fear my Lord and King!

Now conscience-stricken, humbled to the dust,
Doubting himself, in Thee alone his trust,
He shrinks in terror back, for God is just—
    How can a sinner hope to reach the King?

MY KING

O! be Thy mercy in the balance laid,
To hold Thy servant's sins more lightly weighed,
When, his confession penitently made,
    He answers for his guilt before the King.

Thine is the love, O God! and Thine the grace,
That folds the sinner in its mild embrace;
Thine the forgiveness bridging o'er the space
    'Twixt man's works and the task set by the King.

Unheeding all my sins, I cling to Thee!
I know that mercy will Thy footstool be:
Before I call, O! do Thou answer me,
    For nothing dare I claim of Thee, my King!

O Thou Who makest guilt to disappear,
My help, my hope, my rock, I will not fear;
Though Thou the body hold in dungeon drear,
    The soul has found the palace of the King.

MOSES b. NACHMAN.

V

TO THE SOUL

O THOU, who springest gloriously
   From thy Creator's fountain blest,
   Arise, depart, for this is not thy rest!
The way is long, thou must preparèd be,
   Thy Maker bids thee seek thy goal—
   Return then to thy rest, my soul,
For bountifully has God dealt with thee.

Behold! I am a stranger here,
   My days like fleeting shadows seem.
   When wilt thou, if not now, thy life redeem?
And when thou seek'st thy Maker have no fear,
   For if thou have but purified
   Thy heart from stain of sin and pride,
Thy righteous deeds to Him shall draw thee near.

TO THE SOUL

O thou in strength who treadest, learn
    To know thyself, cast dreams away!
    The goal is distant far, and short the day.
What canst thou plead th' Almighty's grace to earn?
    Would thou the glory of the Lord
    Behold, O soul? With prompt accord
Then to thy Father's house return, return!

JEHUDA HALEVI.

VI

Sabbath Hymn

Come forth, my friend, the bride to meet
Come, O my friend, the Sabbath greet!

'Observe ye' and 'remember' still
The Sabbath—thus His holy will
God in one utterance did proclaim.
The Lord is one, and one His name
To His renown and praise and fame.
  Come forth, my friend, the bride to meet,
  Come, O my friend, the Sabbath greet!

Greet we the Sabbath at our door,
Well-spring of blessing evermore,
With everlasting gladness fraught,
Of old ordained, divinely taught,
Last in creation, first in thought.
  Come forth, my friend, the bride to meet,
  Come, O my friend, the Sabbath greet!

SABBATH HYMN

Arouse thyself, awake and shine,
For, lo! it comes, the light divine.
Give forth a song, for over thee
The glory of the Lord shall be
Revealed in beauty speedily.
    Come forth, my friend, the bride to meet,
    Come, O my friend, the Sabbath greet!

Crown of thy husband, come in peace,
Come, bidding toil and trouble cease.
With joy and cheerfulness abide
Among thy people true and tried,
Thy faithful people—come, O bride!
    Come forth, my friend, the bride to meet,
    Come, O my friend, the Sabbath greet!

                                  SHELOMO HALEVI.

VII

O Sleeper! wake, arise!

O sleeper! wake, arise!
Delusive follies shun,
Keep from the ways of men and raise thine eyes
To the exalted One.
Hasten as haste the starry orbs of gold
    To serve the Rock of old.
O sleeper! rise and call upon thy God!

    Behold the firmament
His hands have wrought on high,
See how His mighty arms uphold the tent
Of His ethereal sky,
And mark the host of stars that heaven reveals—
His graven rings and seals.
Tremble before His majesty and hope

For His salvation still,
Lest, when for thee the gates of fortune ope,
    False pride thy spirit fill.
O sleeper! rise and call upon thy God!

    Go seek at night abroad
Their footsteps, who erewhile
Were saints on earth, whose lips with hymns o'er-
    flowed,
    Whose hearts were free from guile.
Their nights were spent in ceaseless prayer and
    praise,
    In pious fast their days.
Their souls were paths to God, and by His throne
    Their place is set anigh.
Their road through life was but a stepping-stone
    Unto the Lord on high.
O sleeper! rise and call upon thy God!

    Weep for thy sins, and pause
    In wrongful deeds, to implore
God's pardoning grace, nor fret thyself because
    Of evildoers more.

Cleave to the right, and of thy substance bring
    To honour Him, thy King.
When saviours then Mount Zion joyfully
    Ascend with eager feet,
And nations shout for gladness, thou wilt be
    Prepared thy God to meet.
O sleeper! rise and call upon thy God!

Whence does man's wisdom flow—
Man, who of dust is wrought,
Whose poor pre-eminence on earth does show
    Over the beast as nought?
Only those gazing with the inward eye
    Behold God's majesty:
They have the well-spring of their being found,
    More precious far than wine.
Thou also thus, though by earth's fetters bound,
    Mayst find thy Rock divine.
O sleeper! rise and call upon thy God!

    The Lord is Lord of all,
    His hands hold life and death,
He bids the lowly rise, the lofty fall,
    The world obeys His breath.

Keep judgment, then, and live and cast aside
    False and rebellious pride,
That asketh when and where, and all below
    And all above would know;
But be thou perfect with the Lord thy God!
O sleeper! rise and call upon thy God!

JEHUDA HALEVI.

VIII

The Land of Peace

Whose works, O Lord, like Thine can be,
   Who 'neath Thy throne of grace,
For those pure souls from earth set free,
   Hast made a dwelling-place?

There are the sinless spirits bound
   Up in the bond of life,
The weary there new strength have found
   The weak have rest from strife.

Sweet peace and calm their spirits bless,
   Who reach that heavenly home,
And never-ending pleasantness—
   Such is the world to come.

THE LAND OF PEACE

There glorious visions manifold
   Those happy ones delight,
And in God's presence they behold
   Themselves and Him aright.

In the King's palace they abide,
   And at His table eat,
With kingly dainties satisfied,
   Spiritual food most sweet.

This is the rest for ever sure,
   This is the heritage,
Whose goodness and whose bliss endure
   Unchanged from age to age.

This is the land the spirit knows
   That everlastingly
With milk and honey overflows—
   And such its fruit shall be.

                SOLOMON IBN GEBIROL.

IX

THE HEART'S DESIRE

LORD! unto Thee are ever manifest
My inmost heart's desires, though unexprest
In spoken words. Thy mercy I implore
Even for a moment—then to die were blest.

O! if I might but win that grace divine,
Into Thy hand, O Lord, I would resign
My spirit then, and lay me down in peace
To my repose, and sweetest sleep were mine.

Afar from Thee in midst of life I die,
And life in death I find, when Thou art nigh.
Alas! I know not how to seek Thy face,
Nor how to serve and worship Thee, Most High.

THE HEART'S DESIRE

O! lead me in Thy path, and turn again
My heart's captivity, and break in twain
The yoke of folly: teach me to afflict
My soul, the while I yet life's strength retain.

Despise not Thou my lowly penitence,
Ere comes the day, when, deadened every sense,
My limbs too feeble grown to bear my weight,
A burden to myself, I journey hence.

When to the all-consuming moth a prey,
My wasted form sinks slowly to decay,
And I shall seek the place my fathers sought,
And find my rest there where at rest are they.

I am on earth a sojourner, a guest,
And my inheritance is in her breast,
My youth has sought as yet its own desires,
When will my soul's true welfare be my quest?

The world is too much with me, and its din
Prevents my search eternal peace to win.
How can I serve my Maker when my heart
Is passion's captive, is a slave to sin?

But should *I* strive to scale ambition's height,
Who with the worm may sleep ere fall of night?
Or can I joy in happiness to-day
Who know not what may chance by morning's light?

My days and nights will soon, with restless speed,
Consume life's remnant yet to me decreed;
Then half my body shall the winds disperse,
Half will return to dust, as dust indeed.

What more can I allege? From youth to age
Passion pursues me still at every stage.
If Thou art not my portion, what is mine?
Lacking Thy favour, what my heritage?

Bare of good deeds, scorched by temptation's fire
Yet to Thy mercy dares my soul aspire;
But wherefore speech prolong, since unto Thee,
O Lord, is manifest my heart's desire?

JEHUDA HALEVI.

X

O Soul, with Storms Beset!

O soul, with storms beset!
Thy griefs and cares forget.
Why dread earth's transient woe,
When soon thy body in the grave unseen
    Shall be laid low,
And all will be forgotten then, as though
    It had not been?

Wherefore, my soul, be still!
Adore God's holy will,
Fear death's supreme decree.
Thus mayst thou save thyself, and win high aid
    To profit thee,
When thou, returning to thy Lord, shalt see
    Thy deeds repaid.

O SOUL, WITH STORMS BESET!

    Why muse, O troubled soul,
    O'er life's poor earthly goal?
    When thou hast fled, the clay
Lies mute, nor bear'st thou aught of wealth, or might
    With thee that day,
But, like a bird, unto thy nest away,
    Thou wilt take flight.

    Why for a land lament
    In which a lifetime spent
    Is as a hurried breath?
Where splendour turns to gloom, and honours show
    A faded wreath,
Where health and healing soon must sink beneath
    The fatal bow?

    What seemeth good and fair
    Is often falsehood there.
    Gold melts like shifting sands,
Thy hoarded riches pass to other men
    And strangers' hands,
And what will all thy treasured wealth and lands
    Avail thee then?

Life is a vine, whose crown
The reaper Death cuts down.
His ever-watchful eyes
Mark every step until night's shadows fall,
And swiftly flies
The passing day, and ah! how distant lies
The goal of all.

Therefore, rebellious soul,
Thy base desires control;
With scantly given bread
Content thyself, nor let thy memory stray
To splendours fled,
But call to mind affliction's weight, and dread
The judgment-day.

Prostrate and humbled go,
Like to the dove laid low,
Remember evermore
The peace of heaven, the Lord's eternal rest.
When burdened sore
With sorrow's load, at every step implore
His succour blest.

O SOUL, WITH STORMS BESET!

    Before God's mercy-seat
    His pardoning love entreat.
    Make pure thy thoughts from sin,
And bring a contrite heart as sacrifice
    His grace to win—
Then will His angels come and lead thee in
    To Paradise.

SOLOMON IBN GEBIROL.

XI

SANCTIFICATION

THE sixfold wingèd angels cry
To Him, Who hates iniquity:
    Holy art Thou, O Lord!
    Holy art Thou!

The mighty ones of earth do call
To Him, Who has created all:
    Blessed art Thou, O Lord!
    Blessed art Thou!

They, who in radiance shine, proclaim
Of Him, Who wrought them out of flame:
    Holy art Thou, O Lord!
    Holy art Thou!

SANCTIFICATION

Those doubly tried by flood and fire
United chant in frequent choir:
    Blessed art Thou, O Lord!
    Holy and blest!

Pure spheres celestial echoing round,
With voice of sweetest song resound:
    Holy art Thou, O Lord!
    Holy art Thou!

All those redeemèd not by gold,
Repeat in faith and joy untold:
    Blessed art Thou, O Lord!
    Blessed art Thou!

They who pass swiftly to and fro
Make answer, as they come and go:
    Holy art Thou, O Lord!
    Holy art Thou!

Who seek His law, and testify
That there is none besides Him, cry:
    Blessed art Thou, O Lord!
    Holy and blest!

SANCTIFICATION

The hosts of radiant seraphs call
To Him, most glorious of them all:
    Holy art Thou, O Lord!
    Holy art Thou!

The sons of mighty men declare
His majesty beyond compare:
    Blessed art Thou, O Lord!
    Blessed art Thou!

All they who glorify His name,
With every morn anew proclaim:
    Holy art Thou, O Lord!
    Holy art Thou!

Israel, His people, ceaselessly
Cry as they bend and bow the knee:
    Blessed art Thou, O Lord!
    Holy and blest.

Those shining as a crystal spring,
Chant in the presence of their King:
    Holy art Thou, O Lord!
    Holy art Thou!

SANCTIFICATION

The stranger's children evermore
The mighty Lord of lords adore.
 Blessed art Thou, O Lord!
 Blessed art Thou!

Those who of fire are fashioned, crowd
On crowd unnumbered, chant aloud:
 Holy art Thou, O Lord!
 Holy art Thou!

They cry, whom He has freed from thrall,
And His inheritance does call:
 Blessed art Thou, O Lord!
 Holy and blest.

Pure visions, bathed in endless light,
Declare 'midst radiance infinite:
 Holy art Thou, O Lord!
 Holy art Thou!

Who to the covenant adhere,
The remnant saved, cry loud and clear:
 Blessed art Thou, O Lord!
 Blessed art Thou!

SANCTIFICATION

'Neath folded wings, in cadence meet,
The glorious ones each hour repeat:
    Holy art Thou, O Lord!
    Holy art Thou!

She, who among the nations dwells,
Chosen, apart, His glory tells:
    Holy art Thou, O Lord!
    Holy and blest!

The high exalted ones make known
Of Him, Who fills the heavenly throne:
    Holy art Thou, O Lord!
    Holy art Thou!

They who their God each day proclaim
'Awful in deeds,' exalt His name:
    Blessed art Thou, O Lord!
    Blessed art Thou!

Those who are awe-inspiring say
Of Him more awful far than they:
    Holy art Thou, O Lord!
    Holy art Thou!

SANCTIFICATION

To all creation's King of kings,
From earth, from heaven, responsive rings:
Holy art Thou, O Lord!
Holy and blest!

JOSEPH IBN ABITUR.

XII

Hymn of Praise

O God of earth and heaven,
   Spirit and flesh are Thine!
Thou hast in wisdom given
   Man's inward light divine,
And unto him Thy grace accords
   The gift of spoken words.
The world was fashioned by Thy will,
Nor didst Thou toil at it, for still
Thy breath did Thy design fulfil.

My times are in Thy hand,
   Thou knowest what is best,
And where I fear to stand
   Thy strength brings succour blest.
Thy loving-kindness, as within
   A mantle, hides my sin.

Thy mercies are my sure defence,
And for Thy bounteous providence
Thou dost demand no recompense.

For all the sons of men
   Thou hast a book prepared,
Where, without hand or pen,
   Their deeds are all declared:
Yet for the pure in heart shall be
   A pardon found with Thee.
The life and soul Thou didst create
Thou hast redeemed from evil strait,
Thou hast not left me desolate.

The heavens Thou badest be,
   Thy bright, celestial throne,
Are witnesses to Thee,
   O Thou the Lord alone.
One, indivisible, Thy name
   Upholds creation's frame.
Thou madest all—the depth, the height,
Thou rulest all in power and might,
Supreme, eternal, infinite!

ABRAHAM IBN EZRA.

XIII

Passover Hymn

When as a wall the sea
   In heaps uplifted lay,
A new song unto Thee
   Sang the redeemed that day.

Thou didst in his deceit
   O'erwhelm the Egyptian's feet,
While Israel's footsteps fleet
   How beautiful were they!

Jeshurun! all who see
   Thy glory cry to thee:
'Who like thy God can be?'
   Thus even our foes did say.

O! let thy banner soar
   The scattered remnant o'er,
And gather them once more
   Like corn on harvest-day.

PASSOVER HYMN

Who bear through all their line
   Thy covenant's holy sign,
And to Thy name divine
   Are sanctified alway.

Let all the world behold
   Their token, prized of old,
Who on their garment's fold
   The thread of blue display.

Be then the truth made known
   For whom, and whom alone,
The twisted fringe is shown,
   The covenant kept this day.

O! let them, sanctified,
   Once more with Thee abide,
Their sun shine far and wide,
   And chase the clouds away.

The well-beloved declare
   Thy praise in song and prayer:
'Who can with Thee compare,
   O Lord of Hosts?' they say.

PASSOVER HYMN

  When as a wall the sea
    In heaps uplifted lay,
A new song unto Thee
    Sang the redeemed that day.

JEHUDA HALEVI.

XIV

Morning Prayer

O Lord! my life was known to Thee
Ere Thou hadst caused me yet to be,
Thy Spirit ever dwells in me.

Could I, cast down by Thee, have gained
A standing place, or, if restrained
By Thee, go forth with feet unchained?

Hear me, Almighty, while I pray,
My thoughts are in Thy hand alway,
Be to my helplessness a stay!

O! may this hour Thy favour yield,
And may I tread life's battle-field
Encompassed by Thy mercy's shield.

Wake me at dawn Thy name to bless,
And in Thy sanctuary's recess
To praise and laud Thy holiness.

JEHUDA HALEVI.

XV

JUDGMENT AND MERCY

By the faithful of His children in their conclaves
    Shall His name be sanctified,
Awe-inspiring are the praises of His angels,
And the voices in His temple spread His glory
    Far and wide.

Those who keep His law shall yet again be gathered
    To the stronghold of His might,
Those who fear Him commune, praying, with each other—
He will hear and in the book of their memorial
    He will write.

Let your deeds be fair and righteous—then unbroken
    He the covenant will hold.
He who maketh bright the heavens, He will heed you
And will count your prayers more precious than the off'rings
    Brought of old.

May the tribes of those who worship and proclaim
 Him
  Be uplifted as of yore,
When He pruneth, may He cut the straggling
 branches,
For to Him belong the sov'reignty and kingdom
  Evermore.

May He lead us once again unto the mountain
  Of His sanctuary's shrine,
There to glorify Him ever in His temple,
For our God will not forget His word, the holy
  And divine.

At His name shall heaven and earth break forth in
 praises
  With a joy that shall not cease,
And the woods shall shout and clap their hands in
 gladness,
For the Lord our God has visited His people,
  Bringing peace.

From each band of angels mighty in their splendour,
  From each shining, circling star,

Hymns and praises evermore declare His glory,
Saying, 'Praise Him with the sound of joyful
    trumpets,
        The Shophar!'

All the creatures of the universe together,
    Heaven above and earth below,
Shall proclaim, 'The Lord in all His works is mighty,
He is king o'er all the earth, and His salvation
        All shall know.'

XVI

GRACE AFTER MEALS

Our Rock with loving care,
   According to His word,
Bids all His bounty share,
   Then let us bless the Lord

His flock our Shepherd feeds
With graciousness divine,
He satisfies our needs
With gifts of bread and wine.
Therefore with one accord
We will His name adore,
Proclaiming evermore
None holy as the Lord.
        Our Rock, etc.

GRACE AFTER MEAT

The land desired so long,
Our fathers' heritage,
Inspires our grateful song
To God from age to age;
His bounteous gifts afford
Us sustenance each day,
His mercy is our stay,
For faithful is the Lord.
   Our Rock, etc.

O! be Thy mercy moved,
Our Rock, to dwell with us,
With Zion, Thy beloved,
Our temple glorious.
May we, redeemed, restored,
Be led there every one,
By David's holy son,
The anointed of the Lord.
   Our Rock, etc.

Thy city fill once more,
Thy temple-walls upraise,
There will we Thee adore
With joyful songs of praise,

GRACE AFTER MEAT

Thee, merciful, adored,
We bless and sanctify,
With wine-cups filled up high,
By blessings of the Lord.
      Our Rock, etc.

XVII

'Lord of the Universe'

Lord of the universe, Who reigned
    Ere earth and heaven's fashioning,
When to create the world He deig
    Then was His name proclaimèd King.

And at the end of days shall He,
    The Dreaded One, still reign alone,
Who was, Who is, and still will be
    Unchanged upon His glorious throne.

And He is one, His powers transcend,
    Supreme, unfathomed, depth and height,
Without beginning, without end,
    His are dominion, power, and might.

My God and my Redeemer He,
  My rock in sorrow's darkest day,
A help and refuge unto me,
  My cup's full portion, when I pray.

My soul into His hand divine
  Do I commend: I will not fear,
My body with it I resign,
  I dread no evil: God is near.

XVIII

Hymn for the Conclusion of the Sabbath

May He Who sets the holy and profane
Apart, blot out our sins before His sight,
And make our numbers as the sand again,
   And as the stars of night.

The day declineth like the palm-tree's shade,
I call on God, Who leadeth me aright,
The morning cometh—thus the watchman said—
   Although it now be night.

Thy righteousness is like Mount Tabor vast,
O! let my sins be wholly put to flight,
Be they as yesterday, for ever past,
   And as a watch at night.

CONCLUSION OF THE SABBATH

The peaceful season of my prayers is o'er,
Would that again had rest my soul contrite,
Weary am I of groaning evermore,
   I melt in tears each night.

Hear Thou my voice: be it not vainly sped,
Open to me the gates of lofty height,
For with the evening dew is filled my head,
   My locks with drops of night.

O! grant me Thy redemption, while I pray,
Be Thou entreated, Lord of power and might,
In twilight, in the evening of the day,
   Yea, in the gloom of night.

Save me, O Lord my God! I call on Thee:
Make me to know the path of life aright,
From sore and wasting sickness snatch Thou me,
   Lead me from day to night.

We are like clay within Thy hand, O Lord!
Forgive us all our sins, both grave and light,
And day shall unto day pour forth the word
   And night declare to night.

CONCLUSION OF THE SABBATH

May He Who sets the holy and profane
Apart, blot out our sins before His sight,
And make our numbers as the sand again,
   And as the stars of night.

XIX

GOD AND MAN

O LORD! I will declare
Thy holy name, Thy glories past compare:
My tongue shall not conceal, O Lord!
Thy righteousness made known to me:
I heard and I believed Thy word,
I will not ask presumptuously.
For should the vase of clay
'What doest thou?' unto its maker say?
Him have I sought and known,
A rock of strength, a tower of might, -
Resplendent as the glorious light,
Without or veil or covering, radiant shown:
Exalted, magnified,
        Extolled and glorified.

The heavens from hour to hour
Declare Thy wondrous works, proclaim Thy power

GOD AND MAN

Sunrise and sunset, still the same
Prostrate in awe eternally.
The angels pass through flood and flame
As unto Thee they testify;
Thy praise they celebrate,
O! Thou, the fruit of lips who dost create.
For Thou uphold'st alone,
Unwearied and invisible,
The depths, the heights, where move and dwell
The living creatures and the heavenly throne:
Exalted, magnified,
      Extolled and glorified.

Who has the glory praised
Fitly of Him, Whose word the heavens upraised?
The Eternal One, Who dwells concealed
In His exalted heights, but yet
In Zion's temple, full revealed,
Did erst His glorious presence set,
And He showed visions then
To cause His image to be seen of men;
Yet past all measuring

His wisdom is, past depth and height
He flashes on His prophet's sight
In visions only as the heavenly king:
Exalted, magnified,
      Extolled and glorified.

His power, exceeding great,
Is without end: who can His praise narrate?
Happy the man, who testifies
Unto His greatness manifold,
Whose faith in God unshaken lies,
In God, whose arms the world uphold,
Who, fearing God, can trust
In Him, acknowledging His deeds are just,
That for himself has He
Made all His works, His creatures all,
And that His awful day will call
All men, the judgment of their deeds to see:
Exalted, magnified,
      Extolled and glorified.

Do thou then heed and learn,
Prepare thyself thy nature to discern.

GOD AND MAN

See whence thou comest, what thou art,
And who created thee and taught
Thee knowledge, and in every part
Of thee the power of motion wrought.
Mark then God's might untold,
And rouse thyself His wonders to behold.
But to Himself concealed
Dare not to stretch thy hand, for then
Thou seekest, with presumptuous ken,
The first and last, the hidden and revealed:
Exalted, magnified,
    Extolled and glorified.

JEHUDA HALEVI.

XX

Hymn for Tabernacles

Thy praise, O Lord! will I proclaim
In hymns unto Thy glorious name.
O! thou Redeemer, Lord and King,
Redemption to Thy faithful bring!
Before Thine altar they rejoice
With branch of palm and myrtle stem,
To Thee they raise the prayful voice—
Have mercy, save and prosper them.

Mayst Thou, in mercy manifold,
Dear unto Thee Thy people hold,
When at Thy gate they bend the knee,
And worship and acknowledge Thee.
Do Thou their heart's desire fulfil,
Rejoice with them in love this day,
Forgive their sins and thoughts of ill,
And their transgressions cast away.

They overflow with prayer and praise
To Him, Who knows the future days.
Have mercy Thou, and hear the prayer
Of those who palms and myrtles bear.
Thee day and night they sanctify,
And in perpetual song adore;
Like to the heavenly hosts they cry:
' Blessed art Thou for evermore.'

ELEAZAR b. JACOB KALIR.

XXI

Hymn for Pentecost

When Thou didst descend upon Sinai's mountain,
It trembled and shook 'neath Thy mighty hand,
And the rocks were moved by Thy power and splendour;
How then can my spirit before Thee stand
On the day when darkness o'erspread the heavens,
And the sun was hidden at Thy command?
The angels of God for Thy great name's worship,
Are ranged before Thee, a shining band,
And the children of men are waiting ever
Thy mercies unnumbered as grains of sand;
The law they received from the mouth of Thy glory,
They learn and consider and understand.
O! accept Thou their song and rejoice in their gladness,
Who proclaim Thy glory in every land.

JEHUDA HALEVI.

XXII

Hymn of Glory

Sweet hymns and songs will I indite
To sing of Thee by day and night,
Of Thee, Who art my soul's delight.

How doth my soul within me yearn
Beneath Thy shadow to return,
Thy secret mysteries to learn.

And even while yet Thy glory fires
My words, and hymns of praise inspires,
Thy love it is my heart desires.

Therefore I will of Thee relate
All glorious things, and celebrate
In songs of love Thy name most great.

HYMN OF GLORY

Thy glory shall my discourse be,
In images I picture Thee,
Although Thyself I cannot see.

In mystic utterances alone,
By prophet and by seer made known,
Hast Thou Thy radiant glory shown.

Thy might and greatness they portrayed,
According to the power displayed
In all the works Thy hand has made.

In images of Thee they told
Of Thy great wonders wrought of old,
Thy essence they could not behold.

In signs and visions seen of yore
They pictured Thee in ancient lore,
But Thou art One for evermore.

They saw in Thee both youth and age,
The man of war, the hoary sage,
But ever Israel's heritage.

HYMN OF GLORY

O Thou Whose word is truth alway
Thy people seek Thy face this day,
O! be Thou near them when they pray.

May these, my songs and musings, be
Acceptable, O Lord, to Thee,
And do Thou hear them graciously.

O! let my praises, heavenward sped,
Be as a crown unto Thy head,
My prayer as incense offerèd.

O! may my words of blessing rise
To Thee, Who, throned above the skies,
Art just and mighty, great and wise.

And when Thy glory I declare,
Do Thou incline Thee to my prayer,
As though sweet spice my offering were.

My meditation day and night
May it be pleasant in Thy sight,
For Thou art all my soul's delight.

XXIII

Hymn of Unity for the Seven Days of the Week[1]

I

Eternal King, the heavens and earth are Thine,
Thine are the seas and every living thing.
Thy hand upholds creation's vast design,
    Eternal King!

The mighty waters with Thy glory ring,
Unnumbered lands to chant Thy praise combine,
And kings of earth to Thee their worship bring.

Thy people Israel, for Thy love benign,
Blesses Thy name and joys Thy praise to sing.
Thou art the God of truth, the one, divine,
    Eternal King.

---

[1] The original of the 'Hymn of Unity' is in seven very long parts. These short ones merely give the leading idea in each of the original parts.

II

I worship Thee for all Thy boundless store
Of righteousness and mercy shown to me,
And for Thy holy book of sacred lore
    I worship Thee.

To Thee alone our fathers bent the knee,
And Thee alone do we this day adore,
Bearing our witness to Thy unity.

Thou art our God, Thy favour we implore,
Thou art our shepherd, and Thy flock are we.
Therefore I bless Thy name and evermore
    I worship Thee.

III

I know it well: Thou art all-good, all-wise.
Thou slayest, but Thy touch death's power can quell;
Thou woundest, but Thy hand the balm supplies:
    I know it well.

Nor sin nor grief can in Thy presence dwell,
Slumber and sleep come not unto Thine eyes,
Great God, eternal and unchangeable!

The soul of all mankind before Thee lies;
Thou searchest all their hearts, their thoughts canst tell;
Thou hearest graciously their prayerful cries:
   I know it well.

IV

We will extol the Lord of lords, whose name
Is evermore and everywhere adored.
In songs and hymns our lips His praise shall frame,
   We will extol the Lord!

He is the hope of Israel, His word
A lamp unto our feet, a guiding flame
To those who trust in Him with full accord.

He is through countless ages still the same,
The shield of our salvation and our sword,
And generations, each to each, proclaim:
   We will extol the Lord!

V

Who shall narrate Thy wonders wrought of old?
The utterance of the lips Thou didst create,
But all Thy majesty and power untold
      Who shall narrate?

Thy ways on earth in song we celebrate.
Though none may Thy similitude behold,
Yet know we by Thy works that Thou are great.

Thousands of angels, by Thy word controlled,
To do Thy bidding Thy commands await:
Yet of them all, Thy wonders manifold
      Who shall narrate?

VI

Alone didst Thou, O Lord, the heaven's wide tent
Uprear, and bid the earth beneath be shown;
Thy word the oceans in their boundaries pent
      Alone.

No aid or counsel hadst Thou save Thine own
When Thou with lights didst hang the firmament
And call the hosts celestial round Thy throne.

Thy works, in universal cadence blent,
Give praise to Thee, and make Thy glory known.
Thou madest all, great God beneficent,
   Alone!

VII

Of old Thou didst the Sabbath bless and praise,
Because thereon Thou didst Thy work behold
Completed in the sun's new-kindled rays
   Of old.

Bless Thou, this day, with mercies manifold
Thy people, that in love and awe obeys
Thy word, and chants Thy righteousness untold.

Lord, we desire to do Thy will always!
Make pure our hearts like thrice-refinèd gold,
And these, our prayers, accept as in the days
   Of old.

XXIV

Penitential Prayer

Forth flies my soul, upborne by hope untiring,
The land of rest, the spring of life desiring,
Unto the heavenly dwelling-place aspiring,
    To seek its peace by day and night.

My spirit does God's majesty adore,
And without wings shall to His presence soar,
There to behold His glory evermore,
    At dawn, at noonday, and at night.

On all His works mine eye in wonder gazes,
And heavenward an eager look upraises;
Day unto day proclaims its Maker's praises,
    And night declares them unto night.

PENITENTIAL PRAYER

Thy loving-kindness is my lifelong guide,
But often from Thy path I've turned aside.
O Lord, how hast Thou searched my heart and tried
    My inmost thoughts at dead of night!

Sleepless upon my bed the hours I number,
And, rising, seek the house of God, while slumber
Lies heavy on men's eyes, and dreams encumber
    Their souls in visions of the night.

In sin and folly passed my early years,
Wherefore I am ashamed, and life's arrears
Now strive to pay, the while my bitter tears
    Have been my food by day and night.

Pent in the body's cage, pure child of heaven,
Bethink thee, life but as a bridge is given.
Awake, arise, to praise God gladly, even
    In the first hours of the night.

Haste then, pure heart, to break sin's deadly sway,
And seek the path of righteousness alway;
For all our years are but as yesterday—
    Soon past, and as a watch at night.

PENITENTIAL PRAYER

Short is man's life, and full of care and sorrow,
This way and that he turns some ease to borrow,
Like to a flower he blooms, and on the morrow
   Is gone—a vision of the night.

How does the weight of sin my soul oppress!
Because God's law too often I transgress;
I mourn and sigh: with tears of bitterness
   My bed I water all the night.

I rise at dawn and still the salt stream flows,
My heart's blood would I shed to find repose;
But when my soul is downcast with my woes,
   I will recall my prayer at night.

My youth wanes like a shadow that is cast,
Swifter than eagles' wings my years fly fast,
And I remember not my gladness past,
   Either by day or yet by night.

Proclaim we then a fast, a holy day,
Make pure our hearts from sin, God's will obey,
And unto Him, with humble spirits, pray
   Unceasingly, by day and night.

May we yet hear His words: ' Thou art my own,
My grace is thine, the shelter of My throne,
For I am thy Redeemer, I alone!
　Endure but patiently this night.'

MOSES IBN EZRA.

XXV

THE LIVING GOD WE PRAISE

The living God we praise, exalt, adore!
He was, He is, He will be evermore.

No unity like unto His can be,
Eternal, inconceivable, is He.

No form or shape has th' Incorporeal One,
Most holy beyond all comparison.

He was, ere aught was made in heaven or earth,
But His existence has no date or birth.

Lord of the Universe is He proclaimed,
Teaching His power to all His hand has framed.

He gave His gift of prophecy to those
In whom He gloried, whom He loved and chose.

No prophet ever yet has filled the place
Of Moses, who beheld God face to face.

Through him (the faithful in his house) the Lord
The law of truth to Israel did accord.

This law God will not alter, will not change
For any other through time's utmost range.

He knows and heeds the secret thoughts of man,
He saw the end of all ere aught began.

With love and grace doth He the righteous bless,
He metes out evil unto wickedness.

He at the last will His anointed send,
Those to redeem, who hope and wait the end.

God will the dead to life again restore,
Praised be His glorious name for evermore.

Printed by T. and A. CONSTABLE, Printers to Her Majesty
at the Edinburgh University Press

www.ingramcontent.com/pod-product-compliance
Lightning Source LLC
Chambersburg PA
CBHW031604110426
42742CB00037B/1138